Shays' Rebellion

by Michael Burgan

Content Adviser: Richard J. Bell, Ph.D.,
Assistant Professor, Department of History,
University of Maryland

Reading Adviser: Alexa L. Sandmann, Ed.D.,
Professor of Literacy, College and Graduate School of Education,
Kent State University

Compass Point Books ✦ Minneapolis, Minnesota

Compass Point Books
151 Good Counsel Drive
P.O. Box 669
Mankato, MN 56002-0669

 This book was manufactured with paper containing at least 10 percent post-consumer waste.

On the cover: Daniel Shays and his men clashed with government troops outside the Springfield, Massachusetts, arsenal on January 25, 1787.

Photographs ©: The Granger Collection, New York, cover, 5, 6, 9, 11, 12, 16, 27, 31; Prints Old and Rare, back cover (far left); Library of Congress, back cover; Rare Book and Special Collection Division, Library of Congress, 7; North Wind Picture Archives, 8, 13, 14, 21, 29, 35; National Archives and Records Administration/Our Documents, 10, 22, 41; Library of Congress, Printed Ephemera Collection, 17, 25, 37; Bettmann/Corbis, 19; Burstein Collection/Corbis, 20; Line of Battle Enterprise, 24, 32, 36; Courtesy of Massachusetts Archives, 33; U.S. Senate Collection/*George Washington* by Gilbert Stuart, 38; Private Collection/The Bridgeman Art Library, 40.

Editor: Jennifer VanVoorst
Page Production: Bobbie Nuytten
Photo Researcher: Svetlana Zhurkin
Cartographer: XNR Productions, Inc.
Library Consultant: Kathleen Baxter

Art Director: LuAnn Ascheman-Adams
Creative Director: Keith Griffin
Editorial Director: Nick Healy
Managing Editor: Catherine Neitge

Library of Congress Cataloging-in-Publication Data
Burgan, Michael.
  Shays' Rebellion / by Michael Burgan.
    p. cm. — (We the people)
  Includes bibliographical references and index.
  ISBN 978-0-7565-3850-7 (library binding)
1. Shays' Rebellion, 1786–1787—Juvenile literature. I. Title. II. Series.
  F69.B88 2008
  974.4'03—dc22   2008007207

Visit Compass Point Books on the Internet at *www.compasspointbooks.com*
or e-mail your request to *custserv@compasspointbooks.com*

TABLE OF CONTENTS

A BATTLE IN SPRINGFIELD

Deep snow covered the fields of Springfield, Massachusetts, on January 25, 1787. In the nearby towns of Chicopee and Palmer, about 1,500 armed men prepared to march on the Springfield Arsenal. Leading some of them was Daniel Shays.

During the Revolutionary War, Shays had fought bravely for American freedom. After the war, he settled in the western Massachusetts town of Pelham. Shays and many other farmers in the backcountry of New England raised just enough crops to feed their families. They had little or no money to pay the debts they owed to local merchants. The farmers watched with anger as their neighbors were taken to court for not paying their bills.

Shays and many other farmers in western Massachusetts thought the state government was not doing enough to help relieve their debts. By the summer of 1786, some of the farmers believed they had to take action. Large

4

After the war, farmers in rural western Massachusetts had a difficult time making ends meet.

groups of them met outside several courthouses in western Massachusetts and refused to let officials do their work. To Shays, the men were simply acting "in defence of their lives and liberties." But Governor James Bowdoin and many other state residents saw the protesters as rebels who had to be stopped.

In January 1787, Bowdoin called for a militia of 4,400 men to fight the Shaysites, as the rebels were sometimes called. William Shepard led the 800 or so militia defending

Shays and his men clashed with government troops outside the Springfield Arsenal.

the Springfield Arsenal. Like Shays, Shepard was a veteran of the Revolution. As Shays and his men approached, Shepard ordered cannons fired over their heads. When the Shaysites did not stop, another cannonball was fired right at them. With that shot, a militiaman later wrote, "They then broke … into the greatest disorder."

A little over a week later, more fighting took place in Petersham, and once again the rebels lost. What came to be called Shays' Rebellion was soon over. But the fighting had a large impact on the United States as a whole.

Since 1781, the U.S. government had been based on a document called the Articles of Confederation. It created a weak national government. Some leaders, such as George Washington, believed that the country needed a stronger national government to deal with any future rebellions. A stronger government could also perhaps solve some of the problems that had led Shays and the others

The Articles of Confederation were first printed in 1777.

to rebel in the first place. Soon after the rebellion ended, representatives from 12 states met in Philadelphia. They wrote the U.S. Constitution, which created a new, stronger national government. That constitution is still in use today.

INDEPENDENCE AND AFTER

During the 1760s and 1770s, taxes sparked American anger against Great Britain. The British tried to collect new taxes, and the Americans resisted. The people who opposed British policies were called patriots. They complained that they had no one representing their interests in Parliament, the branch of government that made laws for Great Britain and its colonies. But even if the Americans were given representatives in Parliament, patriots such as Boston merchant Samuel Adams would have resisted the British. He and others believed that the colonists

In 1765, colonists burned stamps to protest a British tax.

had a right to govern themselves, since Parliament was too far away to truly respond to their needs.

Daniel Shays was living in Shutesbury, Massachusetts, when the Revolutionary War began in April 1775. Fighting erupted first in the eastern Massachusetts towns of Lexington and Concord. Shays soon answered the call to join the militia and help the patriots fight the British. Over

Farmers left their homes and families to join the fight against the British.

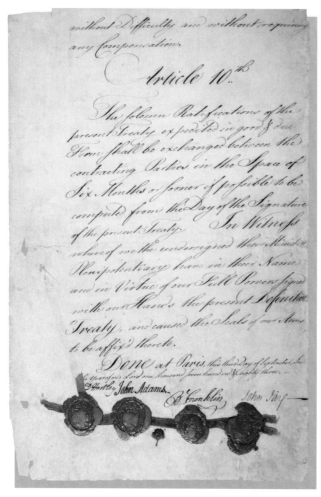

The Treaty of Paris ended the Revolutionary War.

the next several years, he fought at some of the major battles of the Revolution and rose to the rank of captain. In 1781, after being defeated in Yorktown, Virginia, the British surrendered to the patriots, ending the conflict. The United States officially received its independence with the signing of the Treaty of Paris in 1783.

The war had been costly for the states and for the new U.S. government. In Massachusetts, state leaders tried to pay their debts by raising taxes. Most taxes were based on how much land a person owned. Another tax, a poll tax, was charged on every adult male over 16 years old. These taxes were hard on farmers, since most of their wealth was in land they owned. Also, they often had older sons at home who helped raise crops, increasing their poll tax. Adding to the farmers' problems, the new taxes had to be paid in coins called specie. Farmers often traded the goods they produced to pay for what they needed. They did not have as much specie as wealthier merchants. In 1784, one farmer complained about "the great difficulty we labor under in regard to paying our taxes."

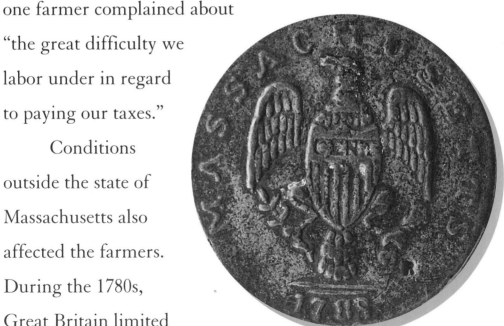

Conditions outside the state of Massachusetts also affected the farmers. During the 1780s, Great Britain limited U.S. trade with British

The back of a 1788 Massachusetts copper cent, or specie

colonies in the West Indies. At the same time, British merchants limited the credit they gave the Americans who bought their goods. In Massachusetts, Boston merchants needed specie to buy goods and pay their debts to the British. They demanded that merchants in Springfield, Northampton, and other western Massachusetts towns pay what they owed them. Those merchants then needed the farmers in the backcountry to pay their debts with specie, so they could pay the Boston merchants. If the farmers could not pay their debts, the local

An engraved trade card advertised the wares of merchant William Breck of Boston, Massachusetts.

merchants often took them to court.

By 1786, many farmers in western counties such as Berkshire, Hampshire, and Worcester faced a crisis. They lacked money to pay their taxes and their debts. If they were taken to court and could not pay their bills, they could be thrown in jail, though few

Many farmers and tradesmen, such as blacksmiths, were served tax writs, forcing them to pay or go to court.

actually were. Creditors wanted debtors to pay their bills, not sit in jail. Farmers who owed money sometimes sold some of their property to pay their debts, but they rarely if ever received what it was truly worth. And both creditors and debtors had to pay legal fees to lawyers and court officials if the matter went to court. To some farmers, the judges and lawyers seemed to be the only people who did well during these tough times.

Many voters in western Massachusetts thought government leaders in Boston were too far away to respond to their needs. Transportation at the time was by horse or on foot, and the backcountry had few good roads. Towns

In the urban eastern part of the state where roads were better and more numerous, people often traveled by stagecoach.

in the western counties sometimes could not afford to send representatives to Boston to the General Court, which made the laws for the state. And the farmers believed the General Court was controlled by the merchants, who passed laws that suited their interests and not those of the distant farmers. In May 1786, the General Court refused to pass several laws that would have helped the debtors.

Still, in many of the backcountry towns, residents hoped the lawmakers would address their problems. During the summer of 1786, voters and town leaders in several Massachusetts counties met at conventions. Most were in the western part of the state. These meetings were part of a tradition that started before the Revolutionary War. In 1774, towns had worked together at the county level to discuss the growing crisis with Great Britain. As early as 1781, they held conventions to discuss state taxes.

At the conventions of 1786, the townspeople of Worcester, Hampshire, and other western counties wrote legal requests, called petitions. They asked the General

Court to let them pay taxes with goods instead of specie. Some counties also asked for a new court system to handle debts. In addition, the residents of Hampshire County said the entire tax system should be changed, "as it operates unequally" between farmers and wealthier merchants.

Some supporters of the state government opposed the conventions and the people who attended them. One writer

The General Court assembled at Boston's Old State House, known today as Faneuil Hall.

in a Massachusetts newspaper said they were "secret but active enemies to our peace and happiness." The petitioners, however, pointed to the state constitution of 1780, which said, "The people have a right, in an orderly and peaceable manner, to assemble … and to request … redress [the correction] of the

Massachusetts officials attempted to address petitioners' grievances in a broadside.

wrongs done them." The General Court, however, was not legally required to take action, and it refused the requests in the petitions.

CLOSING THE COURTS

Some backcountry residents felt they hadn't gained much by winning independence from Great Britain. They still faced high taxes and leaders who ignored their needs. And the state constitution of 1780 seemed to favor the wealthy. Massachusetts residents had to own large amounts of property, compared to voters in some other states, in order to vote or hold a political office.

So on August 29, 1786, a group of about 1,500 men from all over Hampshire County marched on the courthouse in Northampton. Their leaders included several Revolutionary War veterans. At least one, Joel Billings, had also served in his local town government. Some of the men carried guns or clubs, but others were unarmed. As the protesters marched, fifers and drummers played, just as they had during battles against Great Britain.

The marchers gathered in front of the courthouse and refused to let three judges enter. The judges then met with

A band of rebels seized a Massachusetts courthouse to protest the state's tax policy.

some of the leaders of the group in a nearby home. The judges agreed to delay the court session until November.

In the weeks that followed, more backcountry farmers and their friends closed other courts in Massachusetts. They began to call themselves Regulators.

19

They believed they were simply trying to regulate the state government—make it run smoothly and fairly—to help all residents. Their supporters included a few wealthy merchants, creditors, and even one judge. Still, most of the Regulators were farmers or the men who worked the land for them.

James Bowdoin

Governor Bowdoin and many merchants, however, saw the Regulators as rebels and criminals. At times, Bowdoin called in the militia to try to turn back the rebels. But some militia members refused to take up weapons against their neighbors. Still, western Massachusetts had some supporters of Bowdoin known as Friends of Government. A few were debtors, but they thought the Regulators posed a threat to order and to the state's whole legal system.

In late September, the militia came out to oppose a force of about 1,500 Regulators who had taken control of the Springfield courthouse. Daniel Shays was one of about 90 men from Pelham who supported the Regulators, and he led the protesters in Springfield. After three days, he and his men finally agreed to leave, with both sides pledging to "go home friendly." But the Regulators soon shut down several more courts, and tempers grew hotter on both sides.

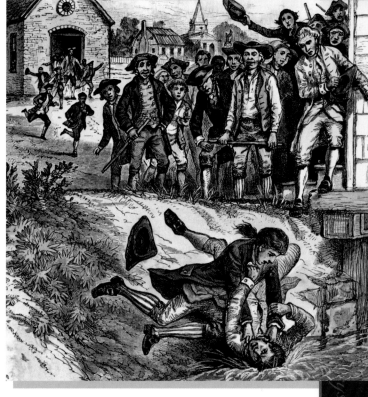

People on opposing sides of the rebellion scuffled outside the Springfield courthouse.

PREPARING TO FIGHT

In October, Governor Bowdoin turned to the U.S. government for help. Massachusetts could not find enough local militia willing to defend the courts, so he wanted national troops to step in. Congress voted to raise an army and asked the states for money. Under the Articles of Confederation, however, Congress did not have the power to force the states to pay. Only Virginia sent money, and it was not enough to recruit troops for Massachusetts.

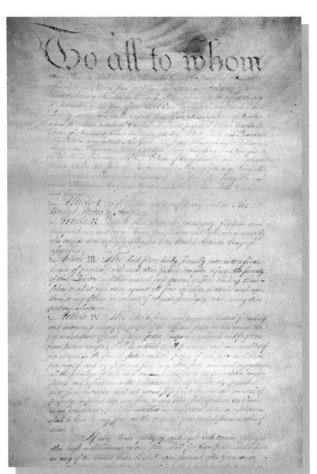

The first page of the Articles of Confederation

The Massachusetts General Court stepped in by passing several laws. It planned to sell state land to help pay for the state debt. Another law also ended some legal fees for a short time. Other laws were aimed directly at the Regulators. Sheriffs and other state officials could shoot to kill protesters who tried to avoid arrest or refused to leave a scene when ordered. If protesters were guilty of breaking the law, they would lose their property and "be whipped 39 stripes on the naked back … and suffer imprisonment for a term not exceeding 12 months."

Some Friends of Government wanted even harsher punishments. Samuel Adams had been a leading patriot during the American Revolution. He had supported the use of force to win independence. But Massachusetts, he now believed, was part of a fair and legal form of government called a republic. He wrote, "The man who dares rebel against the laws of a republic ought to suffer death." But Regulators such as Adam Wheeler said they did not "intend to destroy law, but only to reform all those laws

Samuel Adams

which were oppressive." In November, Massachusetts leaders took direct action against rebel leaders closer to Boston. They arrested three in Middlesex County. In Worcester County, Friends of Government forced people who supported the Regulators to do work for them, or else "they would instantly split their brains out." The western Regulators became angry when they heard about these actions. They also heard rumors of even worse attacks on the Regulators. Shays told his men, "The seeds of war are now sown."

With the national government unable to send

an army to Massachusetts, Bowdoin took his own action. In January 1787, the governor ordered the creation of a new militia, with more than 4,000 troops. He chose Benjamin Lincoln, a Revolutionary War general, to lead it. To pay for the army, Bowdoin asked wealthy merchants in Boston and the eastern part of the state to donate money. About 150 people responded to this call. By January 19, about 2,000 men from eastern Massachusetts had joined the new militia, but the western counties sent only 1,000, less than half of the 2,400 Lincoln expected.

Governor Bowdoin addressed the rebellion in a broadside.

A Clash of Armies

The Regulators knew the new state militia was on its way, so they prepared for battle. Their leaders asked residents to "immediately assemble in arms to support … the lives and liberty of the people." Some Regulators hoped to march to Boston and attack government leaders there. By this time, Daniel Shays led the largest group of Regulators. Across Massachusetts, he was seen as the leader of the entire rebellion, which was not true. No one person led the Regulators. But the forces Shays commanded would take part in the first major battles of the conflict.

Shays knew that General Lincoln was heading west with his militia. Some troops led by General William Shepard were already in the Springfield area to defend the arsenal. Shays and his men marched toward the arsenal, looking for a place to sleep. The arsenal also held several cannons and thousands of guns, which Shays and the Regulators could use against the militia.

Shepard and his men reached the arsenal first. The weapons belonged to the national government, and Shepard did not have permission to use them. He knew, however, that Secretary of War Henry Knox would not object. With Shays on his way, Shepard placed the cannons outside the building.

An engraving of Daniel Shays and his lieutenant from a pamphlet supporting the rebellion

On January 25, 1787, Shays led one of three groups of
Regulators. His and another regiment were on the east side
of the Connecticut River. A third regiment, commanded
by Luke Day, was on the other side. Day and his men were

Shays' Rebellion took place in the western part of Massachusetts.

supposed to join the other two regiments in an attack on the arsenal. Day, however, decided that he wanted to give General Shepard a chance to leave the arsenal. If the militia did not leave, then the Regulators would attack. Day sent a note to Shays describing this offer, but Shays never received it. Some of Shepard's men captured the messenger. Shays began the attack on the arsenal as planned, not knowing Day would not be there.

Even if Day had come, the Regulators faced a stronger enemy. Some of the Regulators marched unarmed, while others had only clubs

Daniel Shays

and swords. Shepard sent out messengers warning the Regulators that if they approached the arsenal, he would fire his cannons. According to one report, Shays laughed at this, and he prepared his men for battle.

As the Regulators approached the militia, cannonballs sailed over their heads. The troops began to move faster toward the arsenal. Then cannonballs began to rip into the lines of marching Regulators. So did grapeshot—tiny iron balls fired from the cannons. Three Regulators died on the spot, and many were wounded. One died later from his wounds. Never firing a shot, the rest of the Shaysites turned and ran.

That night, Shays wrote to General Lincoln. He wanted "all the troops on the part of government [to] be disbanded immediately." Shays also said his men should not be arrested or harmed in any way until the General Court met again to discuss problems in western Massachusetts. While waiting for a response, the Regulators fled north, toward Pelham. Along the way, they raided

A 19th-century engraving of the armed confrontation between the Regulators and the government troops outside the Springfield Arsenal on January 25, 1787

stores for food, while other Regulators left the force and returned to their homes.

Lincoln was not ready to accept Shays' request.

Benjamin Lincoln

He followed Shays north to the small town of Petersham. Early in the morning of February 4, during a blinding snowstorm, Lincoln's militia of about 3,000 men sneaked up on the Regulators. One militia member said the Shaysites "were immediately thrown into disorder." Most of them scattered into the woods, although Lincoln claimed he took 150 men prisoner. Many of the Regulators' leaders fled to neighboring states, with Shays ending up in Vermont.

Commonwealth of Massachusetts

In the House of Representatives Feby 5th 1787

Resolved unanimously that the General Court highly approve of the conduct of Major General Shephard and the militia of his division for their exertions & spirited defence of the Federal Arsenal at Springfield against the daring attempts and attack of the Insurgents

Sent up for concurrence

Artemas Ward Speaker

In Senate Feby 5. 1787 –
Read & unanimously concurred –

Approved
James Bowdoin

Sam. Phillips jun. Presid.

Governor Bowdoin signed a resolution approving General Shepard's actions in defense of the Springfield Arsenal.

In the next several weeks, the General Court passed new laws aimed at the rebels. One gave Governor Bowdoin the power to declare martial law and treat the rebels as "open enemies." Another law, called the Disqualification

Act, said the Shaysites would not be able to vote or hold public office for three years. They also could not hold certain jobs, such as teacher or innkeeper.

From Vermont, Shays and some of the other leaders sought more support for the rebellion. But after the government victories in Springfield and Petersham, many people lost the will to fight. Still, some Regulators in Berkshire County were not ready to give up. On February 27, in Stockbridge and Great Barrington, they attacked the homes and businesses of some Friends of Government. They also took some merchants with them. A small government militia met the rebel force in Sheffield. During fighting there, four people were killed and 30 were wounded. This marked the last major battle of the rebellion, though for several months small groups of Regulators still carried out some raids.

Under a government offer, most of the Regulators who put down their guns would receive a pardon. They still faced the restrictions set out in the Disqualification Act.

Commonwealth of Maſſachuſetts.

By His EXCELLENCY

JamesBowdoin,Eſq.

GOVERNOUR OF THE COMMONWEALTH OF

MASSACHUSETTS.

A Proclamation.

WHEREAS by an Act paſſed the ſixteenth of February inſtant, entitled, " An Act deſcribing the diſqualifications, to which perſons ſhall beſubjected, which have been, or may be guilty of Treaſon, or giving aid or ſupport to the preſent Rebellion, and to whom a pardon may be extended," the General Court have eſtabliſhed and made known the conditions and diſqualifications, upon which pardon and indemnity to certain offenders, deſcribed in the ſaid Act, ſhall be offered and given ; and have authorized and empowered the Governour, in the name of the General Court, to promiſe to ſuch offenders ſuch conditional pardon and indemnity :

I HAVE thought fit, by virtue of the authority veſted in me by the ſaid Act, to iſſue this Proclamation, hereby promiſing pardon and indemnity to all offenders within the deſcription aforeſaid, who are citizens of this State ; under ſuch reſtrictions, conditions and diſqualifications, as are mentioned in the ſaid Act : provided they comply with the terms and conditions thereof, on or before the twenty-firſt day of March next.

GIVEN at the Council Chamber in Boſton, this Seventeenth Day of February, in the Year of our LORD. One Thouſand Seven Hundred and Eighty Seven, and in the Eleventh Year of the Independence of the United States of AMERICA.

JAMES BOWDOIN.

By His Excellency's Command,
JOHN AVERY, jun. Secretary.

BOSTON : Printed by ADAMS & NOURSE, Printers to the GENERAL COURT.

Governor Bowdoin issued a proclamation pardoning most of the rebels.

But those limits would be removed after May 1, 1788, if the men could prove they were once again loyal citizens. The government, however, did not offer a pardon to Shays and other leaders. About 600 men faced trials in court, and 14 were sentenced to death, although only two were actually hanged. About a year after the rebellion, Shays asked the Massachusetts General Court to pardon him. It did, and Shays settled in New York.

In June 1787, new elections gave the Regulators hope that the state government might address their concerns. John Hancock replaced Bowdoin as governor, and some Shaysite lawmakers were elected to government positions. Property and

John Hancock

poll taxes were also reduced. But the new General Court seemed to support eastern merchants just as much as the old one did. Some Shaysites left the state for good.

Others saw their credit problems ease, as Massachusetts trade overseas increased in 1788. Backcountry farmers and Boston merchants continued to disagree with each other, but the threat of rebellion was over.

Commonwealth of Massachusetts.

BY HIS EXCELLENCY
JOHN HANCOCK, Esquire,
Governour of the Commonwealth of Massachusetts,

A Proclamation.

WHEREAS the Legislature of this Commonwealth, with an intention, "not only to adopt every vigourous and efficacious method, necessary to suppress the present traiterous opposition to the laws, and to restore peace and harmony to "the Commonwealth, but also to repeat the offers of grace and mercy to the penitent citizen, and to extend the same as "far as may be consistent with the true interest of this Commonwealth, and the security of her citizens in future;" have, by a resolve of the thirteenth day of June, instant, made provision for the raising and supporting a force, to defend the Commonwealth, against all wicked and rebellious men ; and have also with a very extensive clemency, by the same resolve provided, that, " each and every citizen of this Commonwealth, who have committed any treasons or misprisions of treason against the same, since the first day of June, A. D. 1786, be, and they thereby are indemnified for the same, and for all felonies which had been perpetrated by any of the said citizens in the commissions of treasons, and which are overt acts of the same ; and each and every citizen aforesaid, are thereby discharged of all pains, penalties, disqualifications and disabilities of the law in such case, made and provided : Provided, That pursuant to the said resolve, such of said offenders, who have not taken and subscribed the oath of allegiance to this Commonwealth, since the first day of June, A. D. 1786, shall take and subscribe the said oath, before any Justice of the Peace within the Commonwealth, on or before the twelfth day of September next ; excepting out of the same indemnification, as well all such persons as had been convicted of such crimes by due course of law, as Daniel Shays, of Pelham, Gentleman, Luke Day, of West-Springfield, Gentleman, both of the county of Hampshire, and Lieutenant-Colonel William Smith, of the same county; Eli Parsons, of Adams, Gentleman, Peres Hamlin, of Lenox, Yeoman, Elisha Manning, of a place called the Eleven Thousand Acres, Yeoman, David Dunham, of Sheffield, Yeoman, Ebenezer Crittenden, of Sandisfield, Yeoman, Jacob Fox, of Washington, Gentleman, all within the county of Berkshire, whose crimes are so atrocious, and whose obstinancy so great, as to exclude them from an offer of that indemnification, which is extended to those who have been misled, and are not so flagrantly guilty.

I HAVE THEREFORE, by and with the advice of Council, and at the request of the General Court, thought fit to issue this Proclamation, that the extension of mercy and indemnification offered by the Legislature, may be fully known, to those unhappy offenders who are the objects of it, and who have been deceived by wicked and designing men, and to give them assurances of their indemnification for all past treasons, misprisions of treason and felonies, and of being again renewed to the arms of their country, and once more enjoying the rights of free citizens of the Commonwealth.

As the lenient measures taken by the General Court, coinciding with the wishes of all good men who love their country, and ardently wish for the perfect restoration of peace and tranquility, cannot fail to convince the people of the whole State, that should the unhappy and deluded offenders, the subjects of said indemnity, again spurn at the clemency of government, and continue their attrocious and traiterous exertions to overthrow the Commonwealth, the most spirited and decisive measures must be adopted : And I cannot but believe, that the good sense of my fellow-citizens, the regard the people have for the Constitution of civil government established by themselves ; their knowledge of their true interest ; the obvious necessity of good government, and the unhappy and distressing consequences of supporting government by the sword, will unite all ranks and orders of men, in the pursuit of peace, good order and due obedience to the laws.

AND all officers civil and military, who may be called upon in the duty of their offices to carry the resolve aforesaid, into execution, are hereby strictly enjoined to yield a ready and punctual attention to the same.

GIVEN at the COUNCIL-CHAMBER, in BOSTON, the fifteenth day of JUNE, in the year of our LORD, one thousand seven hundred and eighty-seven, and in the eleventh year of the INDEPENDENCE of the UNITED STATES of AMERICA.

JOHN HANCOCK.

By his Excellency's Command,

JOHN AVERY, jun. Secretary.

BOSTON: Printed by ADAMS AND NOURSE, PRINTERS to the HONOURABLE GENERAL COURT.

After he became governor, John Hancock issued a proclamation condemning the rebels and the rebellion.

A NATIONAL PROBLEM

Though Shays' Rebellion was a local concern, it had attracted national interest as it developed. Secretary of War Henry Knox was from Massachusetts. Early on he had written to Congress to describe his fears of a revolution that would destroy the government in Massachusetts—and perhaps spread to other states.

George Washington was especially upset by the events in Massachusetts. Washington had served as commander of the Continental Army during the Revolution. He did not want the British and the rest of the world to think the Americans could not

George Washington

rule themselves. He wrote, "If there exists not a power to check [the Regulators] what security has a man for life, liberty, or property?" Washington and other leaders already believed that the Articles of Confederation had created a weak national government. The 13 states acted almost like independent nations, not part of one united country. The failure of the states to send money for an army to serve in Massachusetts was one example of that.

Even before the first court closing in Massachusetts, lawmakers in Virginia had called for a meeting to discuss a new national government. In September 1786, just five states sent representatives to this convention in Annapolis, Maryland. The men there called for another convention in May 1787. In between those two meetings, Shays' Rebellion began.

The May meeting was held in Philadelphia. At this Constitutional Convention, leaders who favored a stronger national government referred to Shays' Rebellion. James Madison wrote large parts of the Constitution. He

Founding Fathers James Madison (left), Benjamin Franklin, and George Washington were greeted enthusiastically at the Constitutional Convention in September 1787.

believed that the problems in Massachusetts "admonished [warned] all the states of the danger to which they were exposed." Only a strong national government would end those dangers. In September, the convention approved the Constitution, which created that new stronger government.

With approval from the states, the new government began working in 1789.

The events in Massachusetts did not directly lead to the call for a stronger national government. But violence there and the fear of more rebellions did boost support

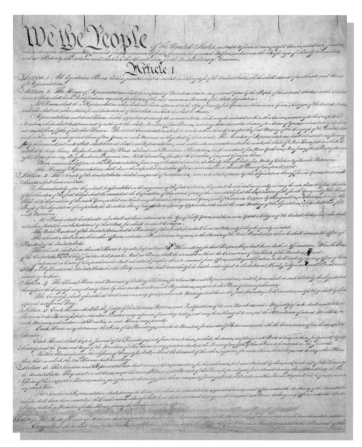

The Constitution is the primary governing document of the United States of America.

for the Constitution and the government it created. Shays' Rebellion also reflected the belief that Americans had a right to speak up when they thought their government was not serving their interests.

41

GLOSSARY

arsenal—storehouse of weapons and ammunition

backcountry—remote areas far from major towns and business activity

broadside—advertisement or public notice printed on one side of a large sheet of paper for distribution or posting

constitution—document stating the basic rules of a government

credit—money or goods lent to someone

martial law—control of a people by the government's military, instead of by civilian forces, often during an emergency

militia—groups of citizens who have been organized to fight as a group but who are not professional soldiers

oppressive—unjust or cruel

pardon—legal forgiving of a crime

secretary—head of a government department

specie—money in the form of metal coins

veteran—person who has served in the military

DID YOU KNOW?

- Debtors in other states, such as Pennsylvania, Virginia, and Maryland, also shut down courthouses to protest their treatment. In New Hampshire, a militia of about 2,000 men broke up protests similar to the ones in Massachusetts.

- Moses Sash was one of several African-Americans who fought in the rebellion under Daniel Shays. Other African-Americans volunteered to join the militia and help fight the Regulators, but state leaders did not want to arm them.

- After the American Revolution, Daniel Shays received a sword from the Marquis de Lafayette, a famous French general who served under George Washington. Shays was forced to sell the sword, probably because he needed money.

- In January 1987, President Ronald Reagan called for a national week to recognize the role that Shays' Rebellion played in winning public support for a new, stronger national government.

IMPORTANT DATES

Timeline

1781 — Some Massachusetts residents hold conventions to discuss high taxes; the government created by the Articles of Confederation takes effect.

1786 — In May, the Massachusetts General Court rejects laws that would help debtors; August 29, Regulators close the courthouse in Northampton; in November, Massachusetts officials arrest three Regulator leaders.

1787 — January 25, Regulators led by Daniel Shays are defeated as they try to take over the Springfield Arsenal; February 4, Massachusetts militia defeats the Regulators in Petersham; February 27, the last major battle of Shays' Rebellion takes place in Sheffield; in May, political leaders from 12 states meet in Philadelphia to discuss the creation of a stronger national government; in September, the U.S. Constitution is submitted to the states for their approval.

IMPORTANT PEOPLE

JAMES BOWDOIN (1726–1790)

Entered Massachusetts politics in the 1750s and led the convention that created the state constitution of 1780; he was elected governor of the state in 1785 and led the efforts to end Shays' Rebellion; he used some of his own money to fund the militia created in 1787

BENJAMIN LINCOLN (1733–1810)

Served in the Revolutionary War and rose to the rank of general, serving under George Washington at Yorktown; in 1787, he led the militia that ended Shays' Rebellion; although a Friend of Government, Lincoln sought pardons for many of the Regulators

DANIEL SHAYS (1747–1825)

Farmer who fought in several key battles of the Revolutionary War; he later became one of the leaders of debtors who wanted help from the state government; during the rebellion named for him, he led 1,200 men in a battle at the Springfield Arsenal; he was eventually pardoned

WILLIAM SHEPARD (1737–1817)

Began his military career helping the British fight the French in North America; during the Revolution, he served in the Massachusetts militia and fought in more than 20 battles; he led the militia that kept Daniel Shays and his men from taking the Springfield Arsenal

WANT TO KNOW MORE?

Further Reading

DeFord, Deborah H. *The American Revolution*. Milwaukee: World Almanac Library, 2007.

Doherty, Craig A., and Katherine M. Doherty. *Massachusetts*. New York: Facts on File, 2005.

Finkelman, Paul. *The Constitution*. Washington, D.C.: National Geographic Society, 2006.

Hull, Mary. *Shays' Rebellion and the Constitution in American History*. Berkeley Heights, N.J.: Enslow Publishers, 2000.

Price Hossell, Karen. *The Articles of Confederation*. Chicago: Heinemann Library, 2004.

On the Web

For more information on this topic, use FactHound.

1. Go to *www.facthound.com*

2. Type in this book ID: 0756538505

3. Click on the *Fetch It* button.

FactHound will find the best Web sites for you.

On the Road

National Constitution Center Museum
Independence Mall
525 Arch St.
Philadelphia, PA 19106
215/409-6600
Exhibits about the history and significance of the U.S. Constitution

Springfield Armory National Historic Site
One Armory Square
Springfield, MA 01105
413/734-8551
Site of the first battle of Shays' Rebellion featuring an exhibit on the rebellion

Look for more We the People books about this era:

African-American Soldiers in the Revolutionary War

The Articles of Confederation

The Battle of Bunker Hill

The Battle of Saratoga

The Battles of Lexington and Concord

The Bill of Rights

The Boston Massacre

The Boston Tea Party

The Declaration of Independence

The Electoral College

Great Women of the American Revolution

Inventions of the 1700s

The Minutemen

Monticello

Mount Vernon

Paul Revere's Ride

The Second Continental Congress

The Surrender of Cornwallis

The U.S. Constitution

Valley Forge

A complete list of We the People titles is available on our Web site:
www.compasspointbooks.com

INDEX

About the Author

Michael Burgan is a freelance writer of books for children and adults. A history graduate of the University of Connecticut, he has written more than 100 fiction and nonfiction children's books. For adult audiences, he has written news articles, essays, and plays. Burgan is a recipient of an Educational Press Association of America award.